Praise for Amy

Dark and audacious. Outraged and outrageous. Fearless and iconoclastic. If Lilith were given a microphone and the spotlight, this is the voice we'd expect. And in her collection *Night Hag*, Amy Baskin delivers exactly that. In music-rich lyric poems, Baskin turns this pre-Eve, primordial woman loose so she can adamantly proclaim that "to love does not mean / to obey." Speaking her mind in both Edenic and contemporary times, this ageless proto-female strives to better our fraught and ineffably challenging world by leading us with feminist wisdom, with "the compass of the womb."

—**Paulann Petersen**, Oregon Poet Laureate Emerita

"*Night Hag* set my loins on fire with empowered carnal eroticism and righteous anger personified through the voice of Lilith, the first woman, who refused to succumb to the wills of man. In light of the overturning of Roe, these poems harken a source of power pulling from a deep well of womb rage, joined with a primal interrogation of the generational traumas and violence against the female body."

—**Kai Coggin**, author of *Mining for Stardust, Incandescent*, and *Wingspan*, host of Wednesday Night Poetry

In Amy Baskin's *Night Hag*, the poet examines, in the most beautiful way, the mythological Lilith. These poems are a perfect elixir for surviving in these times. The images will indeed "grab you by the scruff of the neck". There could not be a more perfect time for this book, as we continue the long and worthwhile battle for women's rights. In this journey of pages, you will find minerals and molecules, caves, burnt rubber on the driveway, a supernova, bicycles and cosmos and a teapot still on the table. This book will feed the soul and remind us, in exquisite language, that our body is "a temple laden with offerings".

—**Connie Post**, Author of *Floodwater* (winner of the Lyrebird Award) and Prime Meridian (International Book Awards Finalist)

Amy Baskin writes with intensity and passion. Her poems reach into your chest, squeezing until you feel like you can't breathe. In *Night Hag*, she takes the mythic figure of Lilith and views the character in modern settings—a timely expression of outrage at the treatment of women in a society that claims to care but often doesn't. Baskin does this masterfully without condescension, exploring both beauty and dread in the world today, all through the eyes of someone filled with past trauma and, yet, a kind of love for that same world. This is a wonderful book, both startling and refreshing.

—**Ace Boggess**, Author of *Escape Envy* and *I Have Lost the Art of Dreaming It So*

In her astonishing collection *Night Hag*, Amy Baskin turns the mythical Lilith into an unmanageable force who refuses be tamed. In a strong, self-possessed voice, Baskin's first woman unabashedly tells her husband Adam, to love does not mean to obey./ You never understood this. She proclaims her right to control her own body: when I feel his child kick within me, I don't want it. She describes herself to a new lover: you think I'm a known quantity/you couldn't be more wrong. With dazzling leaps of imagination, Baskin creates a character who couldn't be more right for this historical moment. Whether exploring the world beyond the garden, linking arms with mothers at a protest, or bumping into Adam and Eve in grocery aisles, this reincarnated Lilith is a playful, sensual, outspoken woman who, in poem after poem, challenges the mind as she engages the heart. And isn't this what genuine poetry strives to do? Cheers to Baskin and *Night Hag* for this stunning collection. This is, I hope, the first of many more to come.

—**Carolyn Martin**, Ph.D., Poetry editor of Kosmos Quarterly: journal for global transformation.

April 11, 2023

Dear Carolyn,

Thank you for supporting me and welcoming me to walk alongside you on our creative journey!

NIGHT HAG

much love and admiration,

Amy Baskin

Attention schools and businesses: for discounted copies on large
orders, please contact the publisher directly.

For information contact:
Unsolicited Press
Portland, Oregon
www.unsolicitedpress.com
orders@unsolicitedpress.com
619-354-8005

Cover Design: Jason Baskin
Editor: S.R. Stewart

ISBN:978-1-956692-56-3

Poems

For Sally and Kelley

who taught me how to love
my body and everybody
through the lens of my body

and For Lilith

the timeless First Woman
who teaches me how to be
subservient to no one

NIGHT HAG

The First Woman on First Love

What did we know of anything then?
We were not there and then
we were.

I don't remember not being,
do you? Before I saw my own,
I saw your own

tender bud. I had no conception
of you, of me. My eyes looked
at your lips, your eyes looked

at my breasts, my belly.
Our hands reached out.
With mirrored palms we

met each other's gaze,
reflecting our hunger
to know more

about ourselves through each other.
I shaped you with my own
fresh hands so I could peg you.

You mouthed me into mounds
that gave you comfort,
unconscious though we were.

Other animals watched us
and we watched them.
We mouthed them, too.

We did take turns at first.
I mounted you,
you mounted me.

We stopped to sleep
and wander through
the garden to feed.

We put everything inside of us.
What stayed down,
we stomached again.

What came up, we used
to clean house. Purgatives
all, senna and castor.

One day I wandered restless
after sex had put you to sleep

but had left me unsatisfied.

I found that tree and ate
from it. The tree that god forgot.
(He later forbade it.)

When I returned I looked
upon you, sleeping still,
and saw we were the same

yet, all the same, different.
I had tasted carnal seeds
and knew

to love does not mean
to obey.
You never understood this.

Subterfuge

stained cloth gusset lined with cotton
traces of lace grace the front face
and flowers so many flowers purple
and pink concealed by the flow no—
the flood of an unexpected collapse of
uterine lining early or late its timing
had slipped off the calendar gone unnoticed
now the search for supplies begins
the furtive quest the bleeding heroine's
journey to escape the attentions of
every major and minor player in this
chapter of her story the dispenser
appears loaded but she has no spare change in
her pockets no will to ask for a loan
because lending grants permission
to ask questions gain answers and
access to classified intelligence so
plan b is to ascertain the degree of the
leak and the damage done from the blackish
burgundy endometrial tide that reeks of dead
fish washed up on a sultry June beach
fold and wad one-ply toilet paper into a
makeshift pad remove sweatshirt and tie
sleeves securely around waist ward
off the urge to slink back to trig unnoticed

they will see through attempts at stealth
coldly calculate that strutting in late
reeking of Marlboro Reds provides the
necessary smokescreen to remain undetected.

"Is it bigger than a bread box?"

That night in high school by the pool when we
all played Twenty Questions, it was finally my turn.

You had changed into your trunks, and wanting
to join in and swim, I chose a word for you to guess.

Was it animal, vegetable, or mineral?
"Vegetable," I answered, certain

that a plant produced the hardened plug
designed to staunch my animal, mineral flow.

"Is it bigger than a breadbox?" you asked,
and since the rules said I could only answer

yes or no, I told you "No," and smirked
to pique your interest. "Is it smaller than a bullet?"

Still, you couldn't fathom a guess
and I wanted to be so bold around you,

so comfortable, make you know me,
and relax in the depths of this knowledge.

I had to spell it out for you, and sweetness,
you were so young and earnest,

you brought back Q-tips from your mother's
medicine cabinet. So, before we swam, I walked you

back upstairs and found her stash, unwrapped
an applicator and showed you how to insert it.

Lilith on Their Mutual Genesis

We were crafted out of the same dirt.
That much we have established.
So if I stink, I'm not alone.
If my sweat trickles sour and acrid
from the pits of my arms and
the backs of my knees,
well, he's no different.
Each time he insults me
he's really insulting himself.

Adam Tells Lilith

You are shaped
like a hollowed out
gourd.

Lilith Reflects on Adam

He smells like loam and mold like me,
but acts as if he's made of stone.

His body is hard.
I've inspected it.
And rough. His face is soft, though matted
with fur of wolf or pelt of seal,
slick when he surfaces.

His body is warm.
He makes heat every night
as I lie with him.

His body is large.
So odd he seeks shelter
within me every night.
I am his cave.
His proper refuge.

A Wanted Child

When my belly, rounded, gravid,
from the seed that Adam planted,
and the blood that stopped restarted
and a head crowned and slid out,

and my muscles cramped and ejected
a frail facsimile of Adam,
I knew that god had had
a hand in this.

God had pulled the kill switch.
And I knew that if god could,
that I could
find that switch as well.

Somewhere in god's creation
lies that lever to shut off
my machinery.
And though at first

I felt disconsolate,
in time, I didn't miss
carriage within me

wherever I went.

Instead, release
of an unburdening. If god
could do this to me and my child,
then, my child, so could I.

Mammary

Adam was betrothed to me
but he was not my first love.
Yahweh, god of war, abba father,
where did you put my mother?
What have you done with her?
You did not birth us,
Adam and me.
We came from mother's soil.

I know you forced her
to wean me, but I recognize
her scent, our strongest memory.
I sense she is near.

I remember crying, hurt.
I remember she removed
a log from my eye
with a surprise squirt
of her milk.
Her sweet, healing liquid,
not bitter and violent like yours
(are you angry I refer to yours at all?
You would have me say nothing.)

What have you done with my mother?
Did you see her as a lesser element?
Are you afraid of sharing credit
for the creation of the universe?
Why do you insist we pretend
you could ever do it
all by yourself?

Her First Blemish

She leans against the car door
his mouth a dumbwaiter
hoists tongue to skin, lips
escalating, trolleying her
guarded rails, more accustomed
to servicing than to being serviced.
Her way has always been to dig

heels in, searching for reassurance.
Her legs shore the weight of her pleasure,
touching ground. Does she love him?
If love is a hunger, he is starving.
She feels him feasting on her,
her body a horn of plenty,
her sweat sweet and ripe.

In the light of morning,
she sees his sigil
embossed on her neck
a branding, an indication
that he samples the cornucopia
then leaves the fields for the gleaners,
discarding bruised fruit.

Lilith's Sex Is Electric

I ride you and the energy I give you is profound.
I am not using you to get off.
I am not making you my tool.
To do that would degrade not only you
but myself and my own actions.
I am choosing you
I am choosing you to
experience me.
The energy I contain.
The light inside.
I am choosing to shine upon you
share my light
light you up.

Can you receive it?
Receiving is a form of giving, too.
It is a generosity of spirit, of time.
If you hold space for me to finish
you are giving me the space to give
you my energy.
You will receive it, yes,
but in order to receive it, you
have to be giving.

Therein lies the rub.
That is the crux of it.

If you can't receive me
you can't wait
then my energy is too much
for you to take.
Like an adaptor that melts
when it can't handle the voltage.

Night Hag

—one of many epithets for Lilith

You want to lie down with me again
But this time pressing my face into our mother's soil.

I tell you no and turn and sit up.
Pouting and frowning, you say I always have my way.

You whine too much. You come every time!
When have I ever left you unsatisfied? Never.

I am not your tool. Cooperate!
Make an effort to help me enjoy this nightly act.

Aren't you curious to learn at all?
Give me your hand. I'll show you how to make me happy.

What's that? You don't want to know? I'm "yours"?
"Yours" only in the sense that you're mine as well, brother.

Possession

—a duplex, after Jericho Brown

I heard you haunt through the bedroom wall.
You shuddered through our father's hollow moan.

You shuddered, making father holler, moan.
You penetrated my wall, entered me—

shrill penetration, my walls, entering me—
holding me gut deep, innards flexed and taut.

Cupping you, your residue, your tension taught.
I learned to share, to retell your dark matter.

You earn my shares, leave my mouth cold; no matter.
You sicken, contagion to young eyes and ears.

Parasite! Embedding in my children's ears.
Imagine: what we transcend we don't transmit.

My breath inhales what horrors you transmit,
then exhales you outside, out their bedroom window.

Self-Portrait of Original Sin

Of course we're flawed.
Created in god's image—
that fucker.
Furrowing our mother,
rutting her fields,
farming her,
grooming her,
spilling his seed,
everywhere.
No wonder his own son
calls me soiled.

Lilith Weeds the Garden

Am I to understand that god created us
in his own image?
Of body, mind, and spirit—
a venerable trinity that most will fail to recognize
again and again?

My body has churned up and spit out
Adam's seed on its own time and again.
This time when I feel his child kick
within me, I don't want it.

My chest pounds. My head rears back.
I will buck this, I will.
Body ready be damned.
My heart is not in this.
Something about this
connection our bodies forged
needs to be broken.

This is a grooming. A healing.
Next time, I will glean the seeds of more
appealing fruit.

I find the outing weed
make a poultice
swallow it, think
no more of it,
then tend
to all I want to grow.

Synapsis

—*Lilith, the sapiosexual*

you know what they say
about a man with big hands
his body is a power tool that
can jackhammer you to rubble
give me a man with a thick meaty
corpus callosum

his mind entwined
his fissure crossed electric
connection between his flaming
mythos his rod-hard logos
Einstein had the largest
neurons

collaborating with violin
and chalk and bicycle and cosmos
give me a man with intricacy who melds
intimate with his deeper grooves receptive
connecting all that's right and left with his substantial
vermis

his midbrain welcoming

each migrating thought no matter
how disparate no walls obstructing
huddled masses crossing vast chasms
I want to wrap my legs around his
brain

Lilith Clarifies Her Terms with Her New Lover

—the angel Samael

let's make this clear
but not too clear
mystery is the elixir that draws us close
but not too close

life is septic transience
do not assume we can
make our relationship permanent
security will be defiled

renounce the illusion of sanitized safety
accept the reality of contagious insecurity
viral threats will outlive outlast and defeat us
you think I'm a known quantity

you couldn't be more wrong
wash your hands
or don't
touch me

life is risk
desire impure

when breath feels too comfortable
when love becomes predictable

remember this
skin cells live for only a handful of days
the cheek you caressed last month is no longer
my cheek

one gene confers resistance
to all illusory protection
you don't really know me
I am not a given

Lilith on Romance

Hover over me.
Don't open your mouth except to
take out your tongue and lick my lips.
They'll dry out soon enough
both lips and tongue
but for now, let's enjoy this together.
This reddening of flesh.
This maddening of heartbeats.
the suck and pull
the tug and release
the young explosive energy of it
that floods our senses
blocks out our ability to perceive
anything outside of our union
it ensnares and
warps the song playing right now
into our song
so each time you hear it
from now on
you'll smell my scent on your fingers
you will rise
and hear me moan
before the final bars.

Amata

Before you tell me
who I am
let me just say
I may wrap my legs
around your brain
delight in the pleasure
incubate your thoughts
make flesh your words
be kind to your beloved
I may wrap my legs
around your heart
gestate what fire you may have
contract my belly hold it in for
as long as I can
give ample time to grow
teach how to feel through bleeding
never what to feel
swear to nurture
separate ourselves from all we create
when our makings are fully grown they are
bigger than both of us
more than we can conceive alone
swear on this

before you tell me
who I am
let me just say
I will never tell you who you are

Samael

—Lilith left Adam for a supreme being

You're an angel to be with her.
To put up with her antics.

We are so grateful to have you
in the family.

We know she can be a lot
to bear.

Her fits of temper, her mood swings,
her sensitivities.

She's always insisted on noticing
the little things in great detail.

When we became a couple,
I knew if I ever left you

I'd be to blame.
My own family would take your side.

If you left me, they would berate me,

castigate me, shame me for my failure

to hold down someone divine.
What had I ever done to deserve you?

Your wings gave me lift.
When you finished, you would

place me back gently
on the ground.

Temporary

When I felt as though a piece of myself was missing
after giving birth,
That's because a piece of myself was missing
after giving birth.

If the transitory nature of my pregnancy took me
from what once seemed a stable frame of mind
to what next felt as manic as
an organ solo
on acid
after giving birth,

Perhaps that's because I felt a piece of myself—
a flat slab of hysterical cake—
form, set, bake
and then
flop out of its spring-form pan.
A birthday ache
that gifted my child life.
Afterbirth.

Severance

Before I even had a chance to say anything,
to the nurse, to the obstetrician,

they looked to your father and asked him
to cut the cord that connected us.

As if the point of birth were to be dismembered
instead of welcomed into our own group.

A slash, a slap, a cry. Your first breath cost
you a penalty, a shot at union.

Welcome to our world, we said to you
and unsheathed the knife. You're on your own.

On bendy limbs untested, I watched
you make your way up towards my nipple.

Launch

To find the calm, to calm
your heart while shock
judders your skull,
untethers synapses
unmoors ships of memories
sinking in trauma.
Cargo containers of words
float adrift, jostled,
seeking harbor
finding no purchase.

When you have lost your mind
and the least amount of muscling
through your day renders
your thoughts a slosh,
you ask yourself while floating alone
in the dark
what if—

your torn nerves never
regain your intellect
your broken blood
vessels can no longer accomplish
tasks you once achieved
on your own?

What if—
you need help?
more help from now on—
to walk, to think, to sleep?

What if at that wrecked moment
you watch yourself launch
and scull through new
neural connections and ask yourself
questions your formerly organized
thoughts never could.

What if your flotsam becomes
your craft? Your brain drifts along,
flat-bottomed, rudderless skiff,
such as it is, over infinite depths
of your calm heart.
Will you reel in this gift?

Lilith Nurtures on the Playground

Dads on their phones.
Their kids running up to me like my own.

People seldom say, "That man is unfit
to parent."

"Play with me!" "Play with me!"
No sign of interest from their fathers.

Seed spreaders plugged into their digital dildos.
Socially acceptable ways to abandon your own

children in plain sight, their bodies
physical proxies for love, engagement, involvement.

I play. Push them all on the tire swing,
help find lost toys embedded in bark chips,

judge slide races. Would these men still unload
their child-rearing duties upon me,

a total stranger, if they knew I have paid to have
Adam's children slid out from within me?

Heresy

—from ecclesiastical Greek haireomai, 'to choose'.

God is not static—
I am.

She changes
like all myths.

Like underwear
should be changed—

an important,
necessary chore

that is only done
in private.

Who says the laws
of nature are immutable?

The speed of light was fudged
by disciples at the altar of science.

I just know it.
Overturn the table.

Question every atom.

The virulence of atheists.

The dogmatic statistician.
The answers are hidden

in the numbers, like bastard
children in the woodpile.

Truth is scattered in fragments.
There is a cosmic treasure hunt.

You will not win the brass ring
on every turn around the sun.

Doubt everyone
who insists otherwise.

Lilith Calls Out God's Rape of Adam

Force him to give birth to her
Make him make more babies with her
Tell him you did this for him
Tell him he's no longer alone
Tell him you know what's best for him

Abandon them to their own devices
Just as they get comfortable
And hope you are not watching
Punish them for disobeying you
Offer no second chances

Intermittently reinforce humiliation
Grab them by the scruffs of their necks
And push their faces in the messes they made
Keep them stained and imprisoned
With the shame you've trained into
The world you have so loved

Bloodshed

I think I know what male ritual bonding
and hazing are trying to replicate:

the thresholds that my body has crossed
at puberty and childbirths.

When men draw blood, they are enacting
a ritual menses. When they endanger life,

they play with the threat of giving birth.
Girls are wounded, tapped of strength for years.

Women and infants both may live, both may die,
or some combination. None of us know

whether we will step through these doorsills
or fail to gain entry unless we survive to tell.

Arranged Match

Extracted from his core, bereft of grit and meal, molded
from his wet rib protoplasm, slick with slop of blood

and pried with force from muscle and tendon. No meat,
not even gristle for a dog to gnaw. The lab jockey shook
that
      bone

like a wand and with it conjured a partner, with tracks of
      veins, tangled hair, clammy
hands and chewed nails. How could he not resent her?

He woke up to find part of himself was gone. He watched
her
      move
from under the tree. He had been asleep and when he woke
      up,

she was there. His side hurt. Throbbing blood warmed and
      spurted
from him, seams loosely stitched, a gross malpractice. When
      she finished,

she undid the rubber hose, snaked it tightly around his arm,
and cooked him a batch with their spoon.

The Rib, an Institution

—a fractured fairytale

God took Adam's bone
sucked squeezed rubbed jerked
the marrow from it
incubated it overnight
and from that jelly
made Adam a father
of a child he had no say in
then god told Adam
have your way with her
this unasked-for creation
not to raise her but
infuse her with more life
in my image
time and time again

Eve's Weakness

They always say she disobeyed.
They're wrong.
Her strongest skill has always been
to follow orders. Rib bone dullard.
She just thought that one time,
god came to her slithering.

Lilith on Eve

Sad little sister
betrothed bone
gristle bride
weak-hipped
overbred retriever
strained genetics
one rib
no coupling
no wonder
childbirth is painful
for you
you are a child.

Lilith Runs into Adam and His Trophy Wife in the Diaper Aisle

He looks embarrassed
and says, "fancy meeting you here!"
It's not fancy.

I think to myself
it's a tired cliché playing out
over a routine errand.

He doesn't acknowledge her.
She's stuck behind pushing
the cart with her swollen belly.

Blink twice if you need
an intervention,
sweetheart.

This time,
did you choose
to have a child
with him?

Upholder

You don't offer any conflict.
You make it easy.

Always stoking his hard ego.
Nice euphemism.

Bring him off, devoted stroker,
magical thinker.

Can you say 'object permanence'?
Adam's not leaving,

Eve, when he storms out of the house,
don't text him your tears.

He burnt rubber on the driveway.
That's a dickish move.

Yes, anger is uncomfortable.
Let him stew in it.

He will never, ever leave you.
Girl, trust me on this.

He's helpless without a partner.
I
abandoned
him.

Acts of Plunder

—a landay on the feminine

whored out trafficked on Backpage and front
page bored into drilled within an inch of her life time

red-tie mothers stand aside and let
the trucker-hat motherfuckers have their way with her

fracking is a water sport toxic
release wastewater burbles back out down her sore legs

putting their things in every hole they
can find or make on her guardians guard her booty

India has granted the Ganges
personhood a river is only one artery

a body spot to fetishize and
objectify she contains multitudes more of them

what of her capillaries and veins
cracked peeling skin and watering eyes her collapsed lung

young girl chin out standing up against
a raging bull alone with no notable backup

mothers stand aside and tsk tsk her

someone should look out for that girl no one cares for her

hands forcing her head into their laps
are you complicit if you focus on all the good

good still exists so simply forget
all that's happening at some point you have to wonder

is she really that worth protecting
could it be perhaps on some level she deserves it

Our River Flows Without Her

—a Cywydd Llessgymog

We let our younger sister down
and now she wears a bloody gown
coat-hanger brown by the bank
of the river rushing by her.
We ruminate on what we were,
remain unstirred; ourselves to thank.

The Compass of the Womb

Lead with the belly not the heart
point poitrine ahead and beyond
and behind, asking who needs
a meal who needs a red warm
pulsing chamber a sensory
deprivation float
who needs to be carried?

That manchild?
That womanchild?
That humanchild?

I set them all down years ago
but not really.

Sure. I cut the cords
and let some die.
I let some breathe, too

felt the warmth of tears
and saltwater exit me
and splatter to the ground

this room cannot hold
these loves cannot fit
and yet

lead with the compass of the womb
chart the amniotic sea
hoist head high
throw out the umbilical rope
in search of rescues.

Over Me

Don't think for one minute
I'm their ball. Hands off.

Don't let them run me
anywhere, skirting opponents,

jostling, fighting
for the skin of me.

I don't need to be a goal post,
either. A temporary object

of desire, a future fantasy,
arms held up in a state

of endless hallelujah.
I can take the weight

of scrimmages, and sliding
cleats and scraped knees,

the bloodsplash
and resistant MRSA.

Field, make me a yard line.
Just one of many,

or a hash mark, or a number.
Some indicator to be of use

to spectators and players, both.
Make me anything that everyone

would need to make it through
the basics of the game.

Lilith with the Long Hair

—for the pregnant protester gassed at the Justice Center in
Portland, Oregon, July 2020

Belly round, mask on
I link arms with other mothers
around the courthouse.

Those vipers won't wreak venom.
They value the unborn life
inside of me with zealot fervor.

My ripe imagined body
is their chosen vessel. They want me
to carry this child—their child—

to term. Shine laser lights
through their visors. All armored
up in there and peeking

timidly through cut plywood den
the size of a speakeasy peep hole.
I wonder

what's stopping them from

slithering out from their pit.
Does my belly give them pause?

Not the young ones. The untrained
weak ones with the most dangerous bites.
They spew poison.

Now another mother
squirts milk in my eyes.
I will wait to see

how well my baby births
in the aftermath. Everyone blames
me. I put this fetus at risk.

They say I should have known better.
They say these men are gods.
I say these snakes aren't men.

Like Trees of Knowledge

Connect me like a tree
with knowledge like a tree
underground and with surety

with surety of years feeling like
a heartbeat's worth of time
leaching out to each other

with offerings of water, energy
nutrition, chlorophyll
like a giving tree

this is my body it will be
given up for you
interbeing starts with connection

from the roots at a cellular level
we grow out of nurse logs, giving trees
nothing grows from nothing

can I see god in a nurse tree—yes
can I see god in the nursling who saps the
energy from the nurse tree —yes

can I see god in the leaders who can't
see god in themselves, sad leaves
they worship sad leaves

Self-Portrait of Woman Discovering Herself

"When the drop cloth looks more beautiful than the canvas."
—Megan Merchant

Don't despair. Know you've made art
in your own special way
and didn't even know it until the end.

Your self-conscious strokes and ratty-ass brushes
that you laboriously retrieved from the back of the
basement cabinet caused you to spill

the turpentine and waylaid you only temporarily.
Your caution and hesitance regarding which colors
blend and which clash

how to feather an edge and how to best define a chin
through shadows and use of Payne's Grey
weren't all for naught.

Your painting is amateur at best,
amateur at worst. Your drop cloth
an unintentional marvel.

Still, you had a hand, and possibly two feet,

in its creation. Go on.

Mount it.

Lilith, Naked

— *"I just wanted them to see what they were shooting at."*—
*"Jen," Portland BLM demonstrator and sex worker,
interviewed on The Unrefined Sophisticates, July 24, 2020*

Broad folds, membranous and adipose,
here, head and shoulders have protruded
curtains parted, knees turned up
against your faces. This is my show now.

You turn away with your weapons,
confused and horrified.
Perplexed, recognizing on some
synaptic level that once

you leave its safety,
you can never return home.
But neither can you target me again
with munitions.

When I'm clothed and standing up
you're happy to forget
my body is a temple
laden with offerings.

The rim of my hip an altar where you
lay prostrate and have preyed and prayed.
You have bowed your head and bobbed inside my temple.
But when I'm clothed you forget where you came from.

When I'm naked here in public, you can't beat me.
You were once nothing out of nothing.
You emerged from my womb.
I am your crucible.

I fill my void with liquid hot and
mold you into weakness, then
cast you out from between
my legs.

I sit before you,
legs spread, masked,
reminding you
of your humble beginnings.

Lady-in-Waiting

—waiting for someone deserving

arched
hidden
in the cupped
cleft of a   curved
depressed dimpled
excavation notched pitted striated
sunken this vaulted void alveolate
and honeycombed carved out
infundibular organ inviolate
convex and   earnest
full and   genuine
you hold   the asymmetrical
truth and tension   of every feigned
forced or   affected unfilled
meaningless   penetration
awaiting in earnest sincerity
with soft fullness vibrating
clangorous truthful joy
every pulsating connection
of substance
so far from
hollow

Turbulence

if I were alone I could take off in rain shower
to land in snow drift and recalibrate

upheaval can serve to reset me there is nothing
like a good cry among strangers in economy

class on a commercial flight I can pretend
I don't mind stare out the window watching

drizzle turn to rain, sleet, snow, graupel and—
All hail!

but this is impossible with my daughter watching
oh, the disruption awaiting her too

she is a barometric gauge when the plane starts
to shake she questions the pilot she senses the change

in pressure keenly it angers her that all could be
anything less than stable she feels the jarring

turbulence I take prophylactic ibuprofen
in preparation for the inevitable migraine

she knows that winter is not coming—it's here
the freezing point suspends me in a steady state

of fear of slipping losing precious ground of thrusting
my daughter out alone in the violent confusion

the condescension of vapor that falls under the gravity
of the current climate the icy jeering coliseum precipitating

there is no controlling the change in atmosphere
from our seats no staving off the discomfort

that comes along with the unknown no way to prepare
for the weather awaiting us wherever we land

Hemostatic Derangement

—excessive clotting or bleeding

What turns out to be essential
in this familiar country
is blood.

Just say the word and blood
will carry water to you
from its own well.

Blood wants to be pumping.
Too much, you say.
But staying silent asphyxiates.

Thicker than water
thinner than isopropyl alcohol
blood can overreact.

Bunch up its fists
stage a protest on the stairs
of your lungs.

Block the entrance
to your capillaries.
You don't even feel it.

It can appear asymptomatic

standing there, close-talking
without a mask.

But express your reservations
and it will type in all caps
on your wall:

"FEAR IS JUST
ANOTHER WORD FOR
LAZINESS!"

Explore
the notion of
therapeutic discomfort.

Molten

I want to tell my daughter
about the stars. That iron that
drips down her legs?

A nun told me once it's our monthly
penance for a crime committed
by the first woman.

What a small story she gutted me
with. We fuse heavy metal in
our cores. We are massive.

I want to tell my daughter
she contains enough
temperature and pressure

to ignite her
bloodstuff into
a supernova.

But instead,
she tempers herself
and tells me.

Lilith's Daughter

Look. He told me to sit down
so I walked out of class.
I don't care whether you call in
my absence or not.
I'm good.

She drops her coat on the floor
and takes flight upstairs
shutting her door.

Sit up, he would say to me.
Now get down. On your knees.
Wait 'til I'm done.

I left that garden lifetimes ago.
The girl is not his.
Her shoulders curve into wings
like her father's.
Her skin takes on a jubilant sheen.

I rub my knees.
The imprint of tiny pebbles still tender,
the meat of my palms stained clay red,
and sit back on the couch.
Finish my coffee.

Above me,
she sings, pen in hand,
as she sketches a world
that agrees with her.

The Sidestep

We are both women in heat.
Perspiration on upper lips and sweat
dripping down on asphalt before noon.

A man with more problems
than he can count
waits for us to cross the street.

My daughter's eyes meet mine
and signal that she's seen him too.
Our bodies, they know what to do.

Together, we give him wide berth.
When he tries to ram her
with his body, we swerve like Ali and he misses.

When his hand juts out to grope,
our hips tack and turn, in a rope-a-dope.
They were made for this tandem dance.

The right of refusal.
The portent.
The pass.

Remind Me

I became naïve, believing growth was linear.
I forgot, for the longest time how we would find
copies of The Watchtower covering our porch
as cyclical as rotting leaves, and spray-painted epithets
on our fences and the walls of our schools.

In one stunted season, they call me baby murderer.
In another, they call my living children demon spawn.
Imagine my surprise each time their circular logic recedes
for a while, like the tide. Then, they call me model mother
and beg me to wetnurse their infants again.

I reach out to you now not to ask for help removing graffiti,
but to ask you to remind me when times temporarily
improve
and I forget again. When I start to spout on about how
there's nowhere to go but up, hand me a beer, rub my
shoulders,
and remind me of what I keep having to relearn—

growth is as linear as yarn. Sometimes it's a fucked up,
useless tangle. Sometimes, it's wound tight into a ball.
But sometimes, you can crochet it into granny squares and
sew them together to make a fabulous pair of pants.

fail you.

—in another time, in another place, but no longer

The metronome of the clock ticks on.
Louder still, the silence—the waiting for you to speak.

Why didn't I have the decency
to clean up the damn house before you got home tonight?

Hadn't even bothered to shower.
Standing there, same as you left me, in my ratty slip.

And you return, hungry and tired,
having closed the big deal, and you've earned our daily
bread

and what was the thanks you got? The praise?
Forty-five more motherfucking minutes 'til dinner.

So the oven gaslight thingy broke.
I could damn well warm something up in the microwave.

But no. I am one self-centered bitch.
And then I had to slip and fall and bust my own eye!

It's a good thing you're here to drive me.
With one eye sealed shut like this? I need all kinds of help.

Get the story straight, with precision.
Once more, with feeling! You know, this story writes itself.

Why do you even bother staying?
After all the ways I have failed and continue to—

Infused

The teapot, still on the table
knows how to keep still. She waits here,
holding hot water and tea leaves,
insulates your brew, works for you.

Defense is not her vocation.
The teapot, still on the table
can't scream or burn you like kettles.
Still, don't handle her swanlike spout.

Thank her whether she's full of tea
or empty. She can nourish you,
that teapot. Still, on the table,
she just wants to keep the tea hot.

What reason, if any, should you
respect her weak and fragile clay?
Can you hold and give and pour like
the teapot? Still. On. The. Table.

Mount of Shards

—a hill built with the ancient remains of amphoras

Once, I was a vessel. Gravid, carrying olive oil within the
       belly of my smooth
terracotta from one port to another. Contents poured out
and
       delivered,
I prepared my hardened hollowed body for the return.
       Handled and emptied,
considered spent, then shattered and left upon a pile,
reduced
       to shards
that clattered on the bones of other broken jars.

Refuse, I surrendered, lying helpless, lost, and still. Silent,
I heard the eggshell clink and wind chime of chipped clay
call
       out
as more of us were abandoned, layer upon layer, necks to
       bottoms.
As numbers increased, I lost my fractured self, nestled
within
       the dregs.

The pile turned into a heap; the heap into a mound and we

joined
our jagged edges together, arm in arm, forming terraces,
        stepping stones,
retaining walls, and caverns to cool and store each harvest
        wine.

Before we were whole, we were broken. Before we could
serve
        together,
we felt worthless. Now, those who are lost climb to our
        summit.
They dance the saltarello, catch a glimpse of vista,
and together, find their place in Rome.

Sweetbay

—Magnolia Virginiana, growing outside the garden

Stooped like a teenager,
shaped like a
question mark.

Not luscious like your cousins—
full-bodied confections
bursting, blowsy Marilyns—

No. Skinny—with once white petals
just past dirty now—but I am not
coming to see you.

I make my way
with eyes closed.
Rounding the bend,

inhaling, you take the pain away.
Out from my neck, jaw,
and shoulders.

Drunk, I wonder how many
other passing noses have peeled
back their masks,

thrust themselves into
your low-hanging cups,
and I don't even care.

On Helping

Before you move to help, be still.
Put down your tools: your shovels, plows,
car keys, laptops, and phones. Stop
chasing the next problem to solve.
Hear your brain chattering, If I only do this,
then everything will be better. Watch that
thought climb the walls, swing from your mind's
caged ceiling. Watch it race around,
picking up, laying down, and arranging—
always arranging! Watch.

Before you can be of use, be useless.
Prone and weak on the floor, helpless. Wonder
how to sit up and stand, and how
it might feel if your neighbor rings your bell
and you cannot move to answer it. Hear
the firefighter's axe hack through your front door
as you lie there, unwashed and unclothed.
Know the difference between the kind mindful touch
and the rough disdainful handling. Surrender.

Before you tell others your plans for action, yield.
Close your mouth. Open your ears. Bare your heart.
Turn off your steady narrative. Your story has no place
here. Tune to the channels of each frequency. Untwine
them.

Tease them apart. Hear the loud, insistent drumming,
the soft breaths so often overlooked. Discern.

Before finding your place in the great library of helpers,
lose yourself in the stacks. Those dusty shelves
contain wonders that have little to do with you.
Give each page attention. Feel their weight in your palms.
Find yourself harder to define. Search for the boundary
between you and them. Question its very existence.
Expand.

Offer the Finest Chair at the Table

what we utter
we infuse with power
staying power
if there's a problem

identify it
out loud with words
the problem becomes flesh
it must be addressed formally

until it is heard
do not let it stand there at the door
without a cup and plate
when concerned parties

refuse to address it
close your mouth and nod
pull out a seat
with air in your chest listen

Pluvial

Like raindrops,
practice falling.

Say, once a week,
just as something we do—

like flossing
or scheduling sex—

it becomes our nature,
like laughing or clapping.

Land and bond,
covalent in our failures.

Huddle routinely
in cold potholes.

Wait for our mistakes
to evaporate.

Fall again without knowing
where to land or with whom.

Raindrops know
they will splash and form puddles

or hit pavement.
We should learn as well.

Expect each sudden misstep,
each pool of blood.

Skinned knees, scraped palms
bear witness to sacrament.

How ordinary, how manifest
to rise up again.

Deep in the Heart

Sometimes someone dies and you look up and notice
the Pacific Gyre has filled the space they left behind.
You think, "How the hell did I not notice what an
unmentionably large space they occupied?" And "Why
is their void filled with plastic waste that's choking all
aquatic life and will never, ever decompose?

What the fuck kind of tradeoff is that?"
and no one appears to be doing anything about it.
Everyone's stymied, mouths gaping, saying,
"Jesus, that's fucked up" and "I can't begin to say
how sorry I am" and "What a waste."

Then you watch them ease off and turn their backs
and run, and you're left with a HazMat catastrophe
on your hands twice the size of Texas. You start to think
you're just another piece of toxic jetsam floating
in the hole your special someone left behind.
After all, everyone is turning tail and running away
from your wake, spinning out of control,

until you see an acquaintance. Someone from the
neighborhood, who waves at you treading water
alone, smiles, looks you briefly in the eyes and then
proceeds to collect one small net's worth of garbage
and remove it.

They leave, but you see them come back. Maybe
not right away, but in a day, or a week or two, and
scoop and paw through the refuse, and take more away.
Your brain knows they'll never bag it all by themselves,
but it gets you thinking

What do you want to be part of—
the gyre
the net
or the cleanup crew, such as it is?

Lilith Returns to the Garden

I know—
it's been so long.
And now

I get the sense I'm still
not truly welcome here.
But I remember

when the powers that be
assured me that I
was a citizen.

"It's your garden, too,"
was the refrain.
We sung and rallied.

Now, as goons lob pepper balls
and tear gas cannisters at us,
I practice Tonglen:

the art of breathing in
toxic fumes and breathing out
nothing but goodness in return.

I hope to change
this chemical imbalance.
At least, I do my part.

You Can Never Go Back

Some very good people watch tv
see suffering over there
and shut it out of our heads
and send up prayers of thanks from
god's chosen ones and think god must want
those people over there, to suffer.
They hold their breaths, afraid to inhale truths.

Some think that when we're baptized
we're protected from and forever
changed in god's eyes, and this
is acceptance. But I've learned that this
is not how baptism works.
The truth is, if I dare to get wet,
dunk my head underwater, and

take a deep breath
when I come out,
I haven't changed a bit.
But everything else has.
I realize the very air itself
has changed, not me.
My duty is to explore outside the garden.

I have a friend as wise as I

(and maybe I'm that friend)
who seldom leaves the state she's in
and when she does, she looks for
signs of comfort and familiarity.
She seldom fords or swims in
rivers and I think I know why.

Leavings

There was a man
no—many men

who touched me
mouthed me ate me.

I swabbed their cheeks
with my tongue.

I see them in my
son and daughter

though they are
not their fathers.

And women, too,
many times over.

Anyone who ever
changed me

has entered me.
I have a gate

with no lock
permeable as the skin

of a cell block.
Molecular as connective

tissue and equally empty.
Stay awhile.

Then pass through me
and the residue

you leave behind—
I will smoke it.

Inhale you until
you too leave no trace.

Back When We Were Dirt

We knew our place.
Grounded ourselves to farms with our husbands' names.
Welcomed earthworms to house themselves within us.

Baked ourselves into bricks, sidled up one against another
until we made floors and walls, slopped on clapboard
with our connective tissues of clay.

We bettered ourselves with sand and gypsum, absorbent
sponges.
Took it all in with room for minerals and molecules alike,
breathed air into the folds of our nostrils and realized we
were alive.

We cultivated ourselves gravid only when we chose
to manifest as arable land. We welcomed the challenge
of tight spaces, parameters in which we carried

our complex creations
formed proteins, and acids, gave footing to
nurslings, and knew deep down nothing good

could grow from moldboard plows tamping us
down to hardpan. Somehow we have forgotten
and let slide that we were always the foundation.

Later, Lilith Runs into Adam and Eve in the Incontinence Aisle

There's an expiration date on everyone.
It's not as though she's a child anymore.
She's more similar to you now.
She's made of the same stuff as you,
raised on your films, the same narratives.
Had your *Tiger Beat* centerfold
plastered to her bedroom closet door.
When you tried to harness the power
of a ten-ton city bus with its failed
brakes and strained gas pedal,

she would come at the thought of you,
saving all those people for her.
And she fantasized about being yours.
She replayed this scene in her head,
pinching her nipples, tongue
out of mouth again and again.
That day when you awoke
and found her lying beside you unconscious,
you saw the life leaking out of yourself
and wanted her to contain it for you.

But neither you nor she could imagine where
the story could go from there.
And now here you are together
squinting and grasping your coupons
shopping for plant-based dairy
substitutes and Desitin and
CBD cream she will massage on your
lower back, right hip
and phantom rib pain
where your arthritis aches most evenings.

The older you get, the more I realize
you're starting to look alike.
And a decade difference
means next to nothing
when even she grabs for her readers
on the bedstand each night to watch
the latest Colbert clip with you.
God, the passage of time
makes my heart soften.
I love you both.

ACKNOWLEDGEMENTS

I gratefully acknowledge the editors of the publications in which these poems first appeared, sometimes in earlier forms:

Alchemy: "Lilith Weeds the Garden"
apt Online: "Turbulence"
Califragile: "Infused"
Isacoustic: "Like Trees of Knowledge," "Lilith on Eve"
Juke Joint: "Heresy"
The Midwest Quarterly: "Bloodshed"
The Opiate: "Lilith Runs into Adam and His Trophy Wife in the Diaper Aisle," "Lilith Nurtures on the Playground," "Lilith's Daughter," "Later, Lilith Runs into Adam and Eve in the Incontinence Aisle"
Panoply: "Subterfuge"
Petrichor: "Lady-in-Waiting"
Pirene's Fountain: "Back When We Were Dirt"
Poetry Quarterly: "Synapsis"
Quail Bell: "Arranged Match"
Rat's Ass Review: "The Rib, an Institution"
River Heron Review: "Acts of Plunder," "Our River Flows Without Her"
Sein und Werden: "Temporary"
SWWIM: "Sweetbay"

Turnpike: "Pluvial"
Visual Verse: "Over Me"
VoiceCatcher: "Amata"

"Synapsis" and "Temporary" appeared in my chapbook *Hysterical Cake* (Dancing Girl Press, 2021).

"Hemostatic Derangement" appeared in */ păn | dé | mïk / 2020: An Anthology of Pandemic Poems by Oregon Poetry Association Members*, ed. Dale Champlin (OPA, Portland, 2021), p.17.

"Mount of Shards" and "On Helping" were written for *Ninety-nine Girlfriends: Collective Giving for Impact* and presented at their 2019 Engagement Party at The Redd in Portland, Oregon.

SPECIAL THANKS

Thank you to everyone for supporting my creative journey, especially the following who teach me through their actions how to be artists, literary citizens, jokers, nurturers, performers, humans. You mean more than you know.

Jason Baskin, Noah Baskin, Talia Baskin, Cecilia Palmer, Allison Parker, my squad. Bob, Jackie, Sally, Matt, Dorin, Adelaide, Lachlan, Maureen, Calvin, Andrew, Ben, Maria, Joseph, Winna, Theo, Jim, Gayle, Jeff, Amanda, Henry, Lucian, and all my family. All of you. Megan Merchant, Jennifer Givhan, Alicia Elkort, Rebecca Aronson, Lauren K. Carlson, Eileen Murphy, and all the Candles. Kai Coggin, Connie Post, Jen Karetnick, Kashiana Singh, Cristina Raskopf Norcross and all the Wednesday Night Poets. Emily Whitman and Holly Westlund, my beetles. Rosanne Parry, Nora Ericson, Cheryl Coupe, Barb Liles, Michael Gilmartin, Cliff Lehman, Robin Herrera, and Lyra Knierim, my critique group. Chelsea Biondolillo, Emme Lund, Sterling Cunio, Stacy Brewster, Jennifer Perrine, my Literary Arts "fellows." Kelley Alison Smith, Sam & Carson Cole, Nalini Jones, Alyssa Lodewick, Ester Eichler, John Spiegelman, Eric Patton, Erin Duffey, Amy Eslinger, Pierre & Germaine Seyt. Donald James Martin, my pen pals. Kendra Lodewick, Nico Larco, Paula Gagnon, Steve Gagnon, Mary Wells Pope, Sam Gartrell, Maya Petersen, Sarah Kline, Elona Landau, Christine Bauer, Tim Campbell, Michelle Campbell, Amy

Williams, Craig Williams, Yer Za Vue, Choo Shiu Ling, Toyama Manami, Miyake "San-Chan" Tomiki, Kagawa Etsuko, Jeff Parker, Jill Powell. Ken Nourse, Marie-Françoise Taggart, Jean Strong, Michael Campbell. Sif Thorgeirsson, Katie Robson, Stefan Hall, David Leeming, Christine Velure Roholt, David Walker, Kimi Walker, James Gannon, Aaron Sutherland, Thomas Reardon.

Paulann Petersen, Dale Champlin, Allison Joseph, Jeremy Manier, Roxas Chua, Carolyn Martin, Nastashia Minto, Steve Arndt, Leah Baer, Courtenay Hameister, Ace Boggess, Deborah Jacobs, Amy Wray Irish, John Miller, Rebecca Smolen, Dan Raphael, Devon Balwit, Rachel Custer, Jerry Harp, Moira Mcauliffe, RV Branham, Jessica Meza-Torres, Susan Leslie Moore, Jen Violi, Carol Schraeder, Ben Westervelt, Donna Hilbert, Corey van Landingham, Kit Graf, Arianna Fiore, Malavika Arun, Mary Szybist, Pauls Toutonghi, Don Waters, Claudia Nadine, Kurt Fosso, Will Pritchard, Rishona Zimring, Mike Mirabile, Mo Healy, Karen Gross, and all of you I haven't yet acknowledged by name in the back of a book. Yet.

.

I offer gratitude to each of you for your time, attention, energy, and example.

ABOUT THE AUTHOR

Amy Baskin is a Pushcart Prize and Best of the Net nominee, an Oregon Literary Arts Fellow, and an Oregon Poetry Association prize winner. She has led generative poetry workshops for Compose Creative Writing Conference and the Oregon Poetry Association Conference. When not writing, she works for the Departments of English and History at Lewis & Clark College and helps run literary arts programs including Fir Acres Writing Workshop. She is the author of one chapbook: *Hysterical Cake* (Dancing Girl Press, 2021). *Night Hag* is her first full-length collection.

ABOUT THE PRESS

Unsolicited Press is based out of Portland, Oregon and focuses on the works of the unsung and underrepresented. As a womxn-owned, all-volunteer small publisher that doesn't worry about profits as much as championing exceptional literature, we have the privilege of partnering with authors skirting the fringes of the lit world. We've worked with emerging and award-winning authors such as Shann Ray, Amy Shimshon-Santo, Brook Bhagat, Kris Amos, and John W. Bateman.

Learn more at unsolicitedpress.com. Find us on twitter and instagram.

CPSIA information can be obtained
at www.ICGtesting.com
Printed in the USA
JSHW082208300323
39715JS00003B/198